JAINISM IN PALAKKAD WITH SPECIAL REFERENCE TO JAINAMEDU

DR. R. JEYASURYA DR. G. MALATHI

ISBN 979-888591554-0

Contents

Jainism In Palakkad With Special Reference To Jainamedu

DR.R.JEYASURYA
DR.G.MALATHI

Jainism In Palakkad With Special Reference To Jainamedu

Preface

AUTHOR'S NOTE

I am very proud to say that, I am a student of History. History is imbibed to all the fields in the Universe. I have a strong belief that, we should not label it as a study of Raja's and Babu's. It is the study of Humanism that is the need of the day. Here, I have to say few words about Dr. G. Malathi, my student and co-author of this book. She has the keen interest to contribute her level best to throw light on the decaying fields in history. As a result, we decided to choose this field of religion. We have collected authentic sources and thereby attempted to make the history students to enrich their knowledge about it.

Dr. JEYASURYA

I have always been quite interested to study all aspects of History with my ability. This attitude has led me in various ways to find out the truth and facts in different situation, place and forms. Generally, I have much interest in revolution and evolution activities in History, especially in Ancient India. The Ancient India shows so many reformations in social, economic, political and religious life of the people. It is not easy to change one system and instill another one among the people as well as in society, but it has happened, particularly in the field of religion. So I want to take this study as challenging one and research about the religion which changes the ideas and ideals of mankind.

Jainism was one of the popular religions in India during 6th Century BC, which turned the minds and life of people instead of Hinduism. The work of Thirthankaras and the way in which they approach the people of the ancient society and development in the field of Literature, Art and

Architecture and removal of hard and luxury ceremonies and teach simple and easy ways to lead the life in all aspects is unbelievable.

I am glad to write this topic, with my gracious Guide, well-wisher, tutor and mentor of my life, Dr. Mrs. Jeyasurya – who is always encouraging to write notes and keep on insisting to do research in various topics, pushes me forward in tough tasks. Without her support and blessing I could not have completed this work. Wherever I needed guidance she did her best for my success, acted as mother figure in my life. So I thank her for giving me this project, helping overcome the challenges and struggles to complete this topic as a grand success.

Finally, the support and blessings of my parents and brother helped overcome the difficulties during the course of this study. I have to convey my thanks to all my well-wishers for my success.

Dr. G.MALATHI

Prologue

India is one of the splendid cultural lands in the world. The impact of Culture shapes people and their actions and production of material artifacts, including the landscape and environment. India has tremendous history in all the parts of the land. Every century made its uniqueness in history of India. One among that was, sixth century B.C, it was a turning point in the political and religious history of India.

Vedic religion and Vedic society shacked and underwent changes by rise of new ideas, aspects, customs and mind free worship, these changes happened by great philosophers and emergence of new religions which made great religious unrest and disagreement with Vedic religion.

During sixth century B.C, different two religions emerged in different parts of land, those were Jainism and Buddhism. The object of study of this book is to make detailed and clearness about origin, culture, tradition and the spread of Jainism. The aim is to collect details of Jain monuments and its history with proper manner.

Compared with other religions, much research has not been done, so archeological exploration and excavation must be made for bringing out and deciphering the inscriptions and other artifacts, ruined architecture to get more details about this religion.

This book deals about Jainism with both primary and secondary sources; and chapter of this work divided into various parts based on details about Jainism in various aspects. This book deals totally four chapters with Introduction and Conclusion.

The first chapter titled Origin of Jainism in India deals with Origin, Spread and Influence of Jainism in India and its influence in Economic development, Philosophical changes, Conversion of people from other religion to Jainism, literature, divisions and sub-division of Jainism.

The second chapter titled Emergence of Jainism in Kerala denotes about the formation and spread of Jainism, approach of rulers in the matter of Jainism. Along with that, also gives information about Kerala where Jainism still exists, survival of Jainism and benefits of Jainism to Keralites, statues and remaining buildings of Jain temples.

The third chapter of this book deals about Jainism in Palakkad, indicates the importance of the district of Palakkad, where Jain temples and religion still exists along with details of present changes and remaining building status.

The fourth chapter of this book is Jain festival, which is celebrate in Palakkad and adjacent areas, entirely deals about different types of festivals of religion of Jainism and which days are sacred for which thirthangaras, rituals and customs, related with other festivals.

Jainism, changed the minds of people in different ways. Its position and different aspects still continue its journey in distinct manner.

CHAPTER ONE

ORIGIN OF JAINISM IN INDIA

INTRODUCTION

India has unique civilization, culture and heritage, one among that, Unity and Integrity, it reflects in many ways; different religions such as Hinduism, Islam, Christianity, Jainism, Buddhism, Sikhism, exist in this beautiful land. Each and every religion has some specific culture and observance. The concept of Ancient Indian religion was 'Aryadharma or Dharma'. Dharma is most prominent than Religion, with the concepts of morality which includes human justice, rights and duties.

The Religions like Hinduism, Buddhism and Jainism, which were origined and together, constitute the cultural heritage of India. Buddhism got most popularity among layman to landlords and ground to top, but it has disappeared from the land of its birth, but at the same time Hinduism and Jainism are firmly rooted in the soil of India. Even though there was some difference between Hinduism and Jainism and Jainism couldn't reach up to the dignity of Hinduism, somehow the impact of Jainism is considerable in the realm of Indian History and it's all aspects such as culture, religious practices, philosophy, fine arts and science.

JAINISM

The Sixth Century got importance in the history of world as well as the history of India. The Sixth century BCE in the Indian History is known as an age of protest, during this century a revolt was organized against the standardization of social patterns, the ritualistic form of religion, the absolute power of the priest craft and the dead weight of dead culture. A new philosophy which made its appearance as anti-social in form and anti-caste in spirit, it preached pure individualism and spiritualism and also discard the principles of social mobility, inequality and injustice and upheld the sanctity of human intellect and its freedom. It stood for both man and woman to achieve salvation as human beings. The Revolts ultimate aim was not materialistic but spiritual, not the socialization but the spiritualization of life. This spirit manifested itself in the form of religious movement is called JAINISM.

Many of the researchers and organization gave various defines to Jainism, among those, Webster's New International Dictionary defines Jainism as " the heterodox Hindu religion, of which the most striking features are the exaltation of saints or holy mortals, called Jinas above the ordinary Hindu Gods, and the denial of the divine origin and infallibility of the Vedas'[1]. And According to R.S.Sharma, "we hear to as many as sixty two religious sects. Many of these sects were based on regional customs and rituals practiced by different peoples living in North-East India. Of these sects Jainism was the most important, and they emerged as the most potent

religious reform movements"[2]. Jainism is essentially an Indian religion and it is still a living faith in some part of the country and its contribution to the Indian heritage is more significant than its numerical strength. It is an institutionalised religion, sometimes enjoyed royal patronage, it has produced worthy monks and laymen from any society could be proud.

The word Jain or Jaina, is a compound word denoting a person who has given up living or thinking like other men. According to J.A.Dubois "A true Jain should entirely renounce all thoughts of self. He should rise superior to the scorn or opposition to which he may be subjected on account of his religion, the principles of which he must preserve and guard unaltered even to death, being fully persuaded that it is one and only true religion on earth, that is, the true primitive religion which was given to all mankind."[3] In this religion there are twenty –four Thirthankaras or prophets of Jainism and their mode of thinking was progressive, revolutionary and yet tolerant. Every, Thirthankaras gave their constructive orientation to the internal conflicts between religions and at the same time, they strongly believed non-violence, equanimity and tolerance. Among the twenty – four Thirthankara, celebrated Thirthankaras were: The first person – Rishabha, the twenty-second-Nemi or Neminatha, the Twenty-third Parswanatha and the last Mahavira.

Rishabha figures as a great saint of antiquity, due to his queer practice and credited with propagating heretic doctrines which are common to Jainism, he indicated in later Hindu Literature. Sreemath Bagavatham denoted him that, the doctrine of Ahimsa preached by him after performing Yoga for several years[4]. Many historians accepts the tradition of the Jainas who ascribe the origin of this system to Rishabha, who lived many centuries back and most of the historians indicated that, the Rishabhadeva was the founder of Jainism.

Parshavanatha, the Twenty third thirthankara was one of the most important leaders in Jainism. He became an ascetic, after spending his life as house-holder for forty years and took to penance. Lord Parshavanath preached four vows to attain salvation, irrespective of his caste those were: 1. Not to kill, 2.Not to lie, 3.Not to steal and 4. Not to own property.[5]

Mahaveera was a historical personality and last thirthankara of Jainism. He was born in 599 BCE[6] in a royal family of Kshatriyas in the democratic republic of Vaishali (Bihar), his father Siddhartha, was king and his mother queen Trishala Devi, sister of Lichavi Chief Chedaka, whose daughter was wedded to Bimbisara[7]. Mahavira's family was connected with the royal family of Magadha, so it made easy for him to approach princes and nobles in the course of his mission.

MAHAVEERA

Mahaveera, led the life of a house-holder in the beginning, and educated to the highest perfection in all branches of knowledge and art. He had luxury life and married a beautiful princes and Yasodhara, but he renounced his family and proceed in search of truth, at the age of thirty[8], nearly thirteen years, he led a life of self-mortification, severe austerities and deep meditation[9] and remaining thirty years he preached his ideas through wandering one place to another and finally, at the age of seventy two he attained Kaivalya (Liberation from body, death). Mahaveera, totally rejected the authorities of Veda and Vedic religion and he didn't believe the existence of God. He firmly believed the theory of Karma. According to him, man himself is responsible for his present and future. The followers of Jainism adhere to five vows, those are, 1. Ahimsa, 2.Satya, 3.Asteya, 4.Aparigraha and

5.Brahmacharya.

Mahaveera's principles were called as Three Jewels or Triratna, those were: Right Conduct, Right Faith and Right Knowledge.

1. Right Conduct: It means that, the Jains must lead a life of conduct by following the five principles of Satya, Ahimsa,Aparigriha,Astey and Brahmacharya.
2. Right Faith: The Jains must have unshakable truth and belief in the twenty-four thirthankaras and their teachings.
3. Right Knowledge: The knowledge of eventual liberation and of life in all existing thing[10]

MEANING

The word Jain and Jainism is derived from the Sanskrit root 'JI' which means 'to conquer'[11]. Jain means, one who believes in conquering the flesh in order to attain that Supreme Purity, which leads to the infinite knowledge, infinite happiness and infinite power. P.Thomas denoted in his book that, the word Jaina is derived from Jina by which name Mahaveera is also known.[12] The Jainas, however, do not considered Mahaveera as the sole founder of their religion. They trace their system to twenty four thirthankaras of whom Mahaveera is believed to the last[13].

The real cause for the rise of Jainism laid with the introduction of new agricultural economy in the north-eastern India. By that time, economic condition of land had changed highly and Iron implements were made and used for agricultural purposes, which resulted in enhancement of agricultural land and its productions. Cattles were also helped in the development of agriculture, so that, rearing of cattle were very much encouraged. Increase of agricultural production led to the growth of trade and commerce, and it resulted in progress of cities where the population of traders and labour was concentrated. It required changes in society and certain well-entrenched traditions. The Vaisyas, having accumulated wealth and property, were gaining higher social status.

Vaisyas got more importance due to the development of trade and commerce. In the Brahmanical society, the first two beings were Brahmans and Kshatriyas and third one given to Vaishyas, so they naturally, look for some religion which one would improve their status. The Vaisyas extended their generous support to Jainism, because of several reasons. But Jainism not attach with the existing Varna system, because Mahaveera preached the gospel of non-violence which will promote trade and commerce, so that Vaisyas were not held in esteem and so were eager to improve their social status. Jainism spread rapidly amongst the trading community of Vaisyas. The emphasis on non-violence prevented agriculturalists from being Jainas, since cultivation involved killing insects and pests; it also excluded crafts endangering the life of other creatures.Trade and commerce were possible occupations and the encouragement of frugality in Jainism coincided with a similar sentiment in commercial activity. Romila Thaper says that, Jainism came to be associated with the spread of urban culture[14]. The west coast provided maritime commerce, where the Jainas became the money-lenders whilst Vaisyas with the merchandise.

Jainism preferred simple, puritan ascetic living. The Jaina monks were asked to forgotten the good things of life, so they were not allowed to touch gold and silver, just they were to accept only as much from their patrons as was sufficient to keep body and soul together. The most important one thing, which lead the Jainism as accepted religion was, the Jain monks teaches Jain principles to the common people in their own language, therefore people welcomed Jainism.

Mahaveera urged his hearers to give up their vices and follies and to practice the purity of conduct and sincerity of belief which is the essence of every true religion. They neither taught any new dogmas or any new rituals nor a new philosophy. The emergence of Jainism was a significant development in India and went a long way in the reformation of the existing religions.

Apart from as a religion, Jainism is a spiritual philosophy, which capable of enlightening the life of human both in internally and externally[15], one who studied, understand, practiced and preached it properly, it shall make them better and turn their world into paradise where peace, prosperity, goodwill, tolerance and universal brotherhood would reign supreme.[16]

In the history of world, Mahaveera is a single glaring example who propagated and practiced the principles of peaceful co-existence which are absolutely needed in the contemporary human society. There was no words to describe about the light of the truth which obtained by Mahaveera, the attainment of Truth was his own but knowledge and verbal symbols of ours are limited and complete one. Acharya Siddasena Diwakar has aptly said, “As an innocent child spreading his tiny hands indicates the expanse of the ocean similarly a devotee through his petty knowledge and limited words makes an estimate of the infinite ocean of the Lord’s knowledge and glory.”[17]

External and temporal were two forms of truth: The External truth has no beginning and end, it undergoes no change at all, but the change take place only in the temporal truth which enclosed within periphery of old and new Truth of a particular time getting old and useless becomes untruth at another time. The Great men demolish this very temporal truth and establish such truth as suits the age. Regional truth, the truth of a particular country, region or place also a temporal truth, because it's value in another country or region or places it becomes untruth in the changed circumstances. So that great men also recommend the changes in temporal truth according to the need of time, country, region or place, even Mahaveera introduces changes in temporal truth, not in the eternal truth.

Philosophy of Mahaveer is man is greater than God, he was not a theocrat but a humanist[18], He held that, who sincerely follows the path of virtue, conquers his inner perversions and awakens the sleeping divinity, become adorable even by Gods. Man do not bend his head to God's feet instead of that , God bend his head at feet of Man, for that, the only condition is that, man must purify his life.

N.S.Chakravarthy indicated that, "Creation means the attainment of Perfection, of Omnisceience, of Ominipotence of Godhood, of Siddhahood. In no other sense, Creation is possible in Jainism. If Creation means, the making or bringing into existence of something which was not before, it implies the conscious; Creation of something is necessary and useful, or something unnecessary and useless.[19]. Mahaveera by his divine message installs man, wandering in the dark alleys of the world on the throne of God. Mahaveera does not deny the existence of God but accepts his existence in each and every living being.

Based on Mahaveera's view, human race is an undivided social group; there is no difference among the Brhmana,

Kshatriya, Vaisya and Sudra, all men are born in same way and no difference in their bodies, no one is higher and lower, or one as holy and other as unholy, this attitude made insult the humanity.[20]

The Jain philosopher made that exists into two divisions: one is kinds-living and non-living. All the living beings are collectively called Jivas and the individualized of Jiva is called as Atma in the world; it is to be found in associated in the material forms. Karma is considered as the subtle variety of this material forms, and Atma is an embodiment of some form of life, human beings have the power of mental, verbal and physical activities. A vibration makes Atma, subject to Karma which shapes the future. The future of a man determine by his activities of mind and body.

The universal form for judging human behaviour was Ahimsa or non-violence, and the Jaina philosopher attached importance was aparigraha, it means complete restraint on acquisitiveness which manifests itself in the shape of sexual pleasure and amassing property. Everyone in this universe wants to be happy and highest aim is non-injury to the sentiment. So Jains strictly follow this aparigraha for remove their life-pleasures, for maintain the high standard of ethical behaviours Jains involves in code of morality, even common man also involves in this morality, and man's behaviour is to be judged by their standard in free from aversion and attachments.

Mahaveera summed up, the Philosophies that, Our enemies are not in outside, they are within us, the real conquest is conquest with petty self, relativity is true one and absolutism is false, the real solution of problem of man is Ahimsa and aparigraha and not violence and lust, those who wants to win the weapons of renunciation must war against internal impurities. Human race is one, so there is no questions or different between pure or impure, high and low, there are no existence of all powerful God, when individual soul get purification, they became God and man is superior to Gods, and at the same time Men and women are equal.[21]

THE SPREAD OF JAINISM

The significance of Non-violence was realized by the people due to the efforts of the missionary of the followers of Mahaveera; these missionary and devotees spread over the country. Some of the royal followers of Jain religion were Ajathasatru, Udayin[22], and Nanda rulers also followed these religion. According to Narayana Ayyar, "Sena and Nanda were two of the chief titles of the Jains."[23] During the first century BCE, Ujjain became Jain centre, and Bhadrabahu with groups of Jain monks travelled to Deccan for preach the doctrine of Jainism, and Sravanabelagola in Karnataka became the center of Jainism in this period. The spread of Jainism in Karnataka is attributed to Chandragupta Maurya. He gave up his throne spent his last years in Karnataka as a Jain ascetic, another cause for spread of Jainism in South India is great famine in Magadha. Even Jain monks went to South under the leadership of Badrabahu; after fifth century, numerous Jaina monastic establishments called Basadis sprang up in Karnataka and Kings shows their keen support through offering lands.

All the religion can flourish with support of Royals, it suit for Jainism also, Chandragupta Maurya was a devotee and patron of Jain religion[24] and Emperor Asoka's grandson Samprati also followed Jainism and sent his representatives to Andhra and Dramilas for spreading Jain religion. During the fourth century BCE, Jainism spread to Kalinga(Odisa) and enjoyed the patronage from Kalinga king Kharavela; and in second and first century BCE, Jainism reach the southern districts, especially Tamil Nadu.

The period of Kushana kings, Jain religion got important position in Mathura, and in early Gupta period it got set back but it got prestige in the later Gupta age, particularly, Kumaragupta and Skandagupta provided liberal patronage to Jainism. Hiuen Tsang, the Chinese traveller who came to India for gathering informations of Buddhism, also written about Jain monks living in Taxila in the seventh century CE.[25] Jain religion was patronised by Southern rulers such as, the Gangas, the Kadambas, the Chalukyas and the Rashtrakudas, they offered liberal grants to Jain temple and encouraged to encarve the images of Jain Thirthankaras. It reached the city of Kanchi in Tamil Nadu. Siddharaja and Kumarapala of Gujarat were great patrons of Jainism.[26]During the region of Kumarapala , Hemachandra Suri was a prominent Jain scholar.[27]

Later period Jainism split into two sects namely, Shvethambaras and Digambaras, the cause for the split was both groups poses legends of specific incidents, these two major-groups factions were appears to have been recognized as early as the 1st century BCE but Shvetambaras only attended the Council of Valabhi in 453 BCE. The Jain Ascetics divided into two schisms, so they were distinguish among themselves through their dressing, that they should be naked or whether they should wear a white robe. Hence, the names Shvetambara-white clad and Digambara –sky clad or naked. Both schism legends gave views about other sets that, Shvetambara legends regard the original Digambaras as arrogant monks who used their nakedness as a vain display of zeal, which Digambara traditions speaks about the Shvetambaras laxity in failing to observe the true standard of renunciation epitomized by Mahavira. Even though they share the principal doctrine and ideals of Jainism, the two factions possess different scriptures and different versions of the life of Mahaveera. Two schism sects occupied different geographical areas, such as Digambara Jainism rose to prominence in South India whilst the Shvetambaras remained primarily in the north; later after the collapse of Jainism, Digambaras came to northwest of the subcontinent. Today both factions continue their process as in independent manner, although some disputes came among them over administration of pilgrimage and sometimes leads to litigation and even violence.

Medieval Jainism saw the rise of number of sub-groups or Gacchas among the Shvetambaras, these divisions were based on the local communities or adherence to a specific Jain holy man and it got minor difference from origianl doctrines and totally its eighty four such Gacchas but only faction of that number exists today, the most prominent of which are the Tapa-Gaccha and Kharana-Gaccha. The question arose that, whether the practice of worshiping images of saints and Tirthankaras, so one of the sect broken from Shvetambaras, under the leadership of Lavaji the Sthanakvasis, whilst most of the Shvetambaras accept thes practice as an authentic part of the Jain panth- and hence are known as Murti-pujakas or Deravasis-the Sthanakavasis urge that it is alien to the true spirit of Jainism. On 1764, Acharya Bhikshu founded one sect of Jainism,called Terapanthis, which broken away from the Sthanakavasis whom they criticized for worldliness and a lack of commitment, but this Terapanthis later continued under one overall leader or Acharya and maintain its integrity after the death of Acharya Bhikshu's death in 1803.

Amongst the Digambaras, Kanji Swamy, who was monk in his early life in Sthanakavasi Shvetambaras, found a sect called as Kanji Swami Panth. But he realised that Digambara Jainism was close to the spiritual essence of the traditions by the influence of writing of Digambara teacher Kunda Kunda. So he left the Sthanakavasis with numerous followers and founded his own sect with the ideals and teachings of Digambaras, especially Kundakunda. Today the Kanji Swami Panth is an active Digambara Sect, campaigning on various issues, involved in various missionary activities to spread the message of Jainism.

Digambaras followed image worship in temples, but Shvethambaras condemn such practices. During sixteenth century, teacher Taranathswami, farbade image worship, and formed new sects known as the Taranapanthis, which opposited to image worship. One more sect called Adhyamata movement which was found by Banarsidas, it stressed the essence of Jainism was the mystical experience of the spiritual self and the individual realization can attainable by both lay man and monks. But it disappeared within one hundred year after the death of Banarsidas, but the ideas and taught were similar by one more sect known as the Terahapanthis.

Relationships between the Jain sects are complex and varied with the primary division persisting between Shvethambaras and Digambaras. Social interaction and intermarriage is common between the subsects of two main sects. Despite the sectarian divisions, all sub-groups still followed the fundamental principles and even based on geographical location or adherence to a particular spiritual leader, many divisions have occurred.

Augusta Klien says that, the most curious feature of Jaina Asceticm is the great marit obtained by refusing to wear clothes. Great is the praise of the naked monk whom grass pricks, cold attacks, flies and mosquitoes sting[28]. The custom of discarding clothes was at first practiced by all Jain ascetics, the Digambaras or sky clad ones and Shvetambaras or white robed ones, cannot be traced back beyond the sixth century of one era. The custom is falling now into disuse. Some of the statues of Thirthankaras were multitude at Gwaliar, which carved in sandstone rock on which the fort is built.

CONTRIBUTION OF JAINISM

Each and Every division of Jainism made manifold contribution to the increase the value of Indian culture and philosophy, and the basic principles of Indian culture is Ahima, it also popularisation by Jainism, it show various form of life such as kindness and love and the same time it hated and condemned the various types of sacrifices and yajnas and it reflect in the subsequent countries, which result that, they left that practices. The level of Ahima was rising by Jains along with that they insisted non-injury to the animate as well as inanimate objects by speech and action.

Jainism insisted equality among all the people against of caste system, and it purified the Hinduism by removed the evil practice and regain its popularity, by provided an impetus to the Hindu scholars to set their house in order, by this activities it vanish the most of the evil practices from Hinduism.

Jainism, contributed to the enrichment of the Indian philosophy by contributing the principle of Satyavad. The Jain philosophy of dualism were Jiva(soul) and Ajiva (matter) the theory of Karma transmigration of souls, the ethical code and a course of discipline, leading to Nirvana are great contribution of Jains to the philosophical world.

Jainism encouraged utilitarian activist by insisting on greater rendering of greater service to humanity. They were engaged in public works such as, construction of inns, hospitals, schools and other institutions of public utility.

Strengthening of ethical and moral virtures, it contributed much and advocated for rigid austerities in both external and internal. The external austerities include begging, fasting, gradual abstention from food etc. The internal austerities were humility, service, study, meditation, penances and other prescribed ways. Jainism prescribed some ways to individuals for get spiritual evolutions, such as right faith, right knowledge and right conduct, which lead to Nirvana.

According to tradition the original doctrines taught by Mahaveera were contained in fourteen old texts styled Purvas[29]. The council was formed at Pataliputra by Sthulabhadra at the end of the fourth century BCE for reconstructed the Jain canon in twelve Angas or sections, superseding the fourteen Purvas. Most of the authorities were opposite this divisions and this canon was accept only by the Shvethambaras, the Digambaras argued that old canon was hopelessly lost. So another council was formed at Valabhi in fifth century CE for reduced the writings and finalised the existing texts. [30] This time the twelfth Angas had been lost and new additional had been made in another forms, namely Upangas or minor sections and various lesser works.[31] The Jain canon is written in Prakrit language called as Ardha-magadi and this works categorized into six; each divisions carries different principles and logics.

Firstly, Jainism's rules and regulations carry in twelve Angas, with help of legends and theories it explained about Jain doctrines, and rules for conducts of monks. Acharanga

Sutra and Bhagavati Sutra are the most important among the twelve Angas.

Secondly, the twelve Upangas which contains dogmatic and mythological in character, the second Bayapasenaijja has some literary merits and narrate the dialogues between the Jain monk Kesi and King Paesi(probably Kosala king Prasenajit), the fifth, sixth and seventh Upangas contains Astronomy, Geography and Cosmology respectively.

Thirdly, the ten Prakirans (scattered), deals doctrinal matters of Jainism in verse forms. Fourthly, the six Chedasutras highlight, legend's illustrations, monks and nuns disciplinary rules, the best works is Kalpasutra attributed to Badrabahu, it describe about the lives of Jainas schools and rules to be observed by monks, the another Kalpsutra which forms in fifth Chedasustra deals about principal treatise on the rules of conducts of Jain monks and nuns's. Fifthly, the four Malasutras which contain religious poetry, parables, maximum ballads and dialogue, it deals the basic doctrine of Jainism.

The final works, contains, several miscellaneous texts, it not only deals about concerned with religious subjects but also relate with secular subjects like Arthasastra, poetics, Kamashatra etc. Nandisutra and Anuyogadara, a sort of encyclopedic texts were separate canonical texts which contain texts of accounts of the different branches of knowledge of Jaina canon. Niryukts or commentaries of Jain monks, Tikas of Jain writers in Sanskrit and works of philosophy were also include miscanelleous works.

The Jainas have vast non-canonical literature in the form of commentaries, kavyas, lyrics etc. The most famous commentators was Haribhadra, who belonged to second half of the ninth century CE[32], he is reputed to have composed one thousand and forty works[33] some other commentators who lived in the eleventh century CE were, Santisuri, Devendragani, Abhayadeva, Dhronacharya, Malayagiri, Maladari, Hemachadran, Kshemakeerthi etc.[34]

The Jaina possesses an extensive poetic literature, called Charitras and Prabanthas which are mostly didactic in character. Hemachandra, one among the celebrities, who was veritable genius, produced grammar lexicography poetics, metrics and philosophy. There are semi-historical works like Prabhandha-Chintamani of Merutunga and Prabandha-Kosa of Rajasekharan.

Digambaras also produced their literature like Shvetambaras, and those were written in both Prakrit and Sanskrit. Kundakunda was most notable scholar in Digambara sect. G.Jawaharlal aptly points out; “It is beyond doubt that Kundakunda is the most reputed as well as popular name in the literary history of Jainism”[35]. Vattakers, Swami Kertikeya, Yati Vrishabha Samanatabhadra and Manatunga were some other notable scholars of this sect, various sages and lives of Jain monks were dealt as stories by them. Jain literature was also composed in Tamil language, some of the Jain works were Jivaka Chintamani, Silappathikaram, Neelakesi and Yashodara Kavya.

Indian culture was influenced by Jain literatures, the populations of the Jains in India are predominantly found in Rajaputana, Gujarat and some district of the South and Middle India. According to Thomas, the Jains in India at present do not number more than two millions;[36]but their influence in the country is quite considerable. The reason for this is that the Jains constitute one of the wealthiest communities in India.

In Encyclopedia Britannica, in the architecture the Jains excel, though Buddhist models were adopted in stupas and cave-temple, they carried the art of carving in stone to the highest point.[37] The one more contribution of Jainism to the architecture of India is erected the Jain temple in all over South India, and most wonderful conceptions was the manasthambhas or the tall standing pillars in front of most of the temples. No two pillars are compatible, and most of them are seemed fantastic due to ornament. Their massiveness and richness of carving bear evidence to their being copies of wooden models. Temples in various place of India shows their uniqueness, those were, and the marvels of Jain Architecture reflect in The Tribhuvanatilaka Jinalaya and temple at Coorge shows exquisite beauty, the temples at Sravanabelgola, Janathpura, Hansoge and Helebeedu are spacious with individuality of their own. The pillars of Shantinath Temple at Halebeedu have been so polished that the reflection of the individuals looking at them. Convey different figures both in size and posture. Similarly, highly polished and strongly magnetic pillar appeared in Belgaum, the best model for four faced temples were, the Chatirmukha-bastis at Mudabirdi Laxmeshwar and Gersoppa.

There are numerous temples at Aihole, but today there are only in three temples has Jaina images; the most famous one is Meguti temple. The idol of Bhagavan Parsvanath with a thousand-hooded Cobra appeared in the temple at the Daega area of Bijapur; Banavasi and Bhatkal which were ones ruled by Jaina kings have exquisite temples. The place Haduhalli which surrounded by hills which is situated ten miles away from Bhatakal has three temples; one of them has beautiful images of twenty-four Thirthankaras with the most beautiful carved images of Dharmendra and

Padmavati. Perhaps, the images seem to have carved by the same sculpture that made identical images at Srirangapatana situated at a distance of ten miles from Mysore.

Both the temple with Math at Sravanabelgola and the cave temple at Badami bear the witness of wall paintings which are clearly visible on the walls inspite of the lapse of hundreds of years. In the former, a picture of Samvarasarana with Bhagavan Parsavanath preaching the eternal doctrine of Jainism, at the same time other illustrate the Jain concept of lesyas of samsara and other puranic stories. In Tamilnadu, there are some wall paintings at Kanchipuram and Tirumalai, apart from wall painting, manuscripts of Kalpasutra and of Bhaktamrastotra which illustrate the subject by means of paintings on the palm leaves.

All the unique art and architecture would not have flourished in the South or the Dakshipatha if it had not been the strong hold of Jainism. Jainism was patronized and promoted its spread by the rulers such as, Nandas, Mauryas and Satavahanas. The Kadambas and Barnavasi were undoubtedly Jains. The Guru of Ganga Kings, Madhava and Dadiga was Jain Acharya, Simhanandi, and their capital was Kuvalapura which is identifies with modern Kolar in Karnataka.

Peoples, metaphisical and rightousness of their standard of living by Jain temples, caves, Stupas, Idols and pictures, also try to beautify the different parts of the land,along that this vision purified and delighted heart. The position of Jainism in History is very popular, without any aware in the merits of Jainism, no one does not perfect in the knowledge of Indian culture. Jain culture does not give any emphasize in communal divisions. This is the unique feature in international view. The awareness in the goodness of all creatures is more valuable in the present world. The upcoming matters will deal about Jainism in Kerala along with art and architecture of Kerala.

References

[1] W.T.Harri's, Websters New International Dictionary, p.1155

[2] R.S.Sharma, Ancient India, p.72

[3] Abbe,J.A.Dubois, Hindu Manners, Customs and Ceremonies,pp.685-686

[4] Thuchanthu Ramanujan Ezhuthachan, Sreemath Bagavatham, p.48

[5] R.S.Tripathi, History of Ancient India,p.97

[6] Ramesh Chandra, Religious of India,p.265

[7] All India Chinmaya Yuvakendra, Aakening Indians to India,p.321

[8] Romila Thaper, A History of India, vol.I, p.64

[9] Manak Chand Jaini, Life of Mahavira,p.42

[10] Ibid,p.26

[11] Lewis Browne, This Believing World,p.130

[12] P.Thomas, Festivals and Holidays of India,p.74

[13] P.Thomas, Hindu Religion Customs and Manners,p.48

[14] Romila Thaper,op.cit,p.65

[15] R.M.Das, Jainism A Study,p.9

[16] Ibid.p.9

[17] R.M.Das, op.cit,p.147

[18] R.M.Das, op.cit,p.149

[19] Nemichandra Siddhanta Chakravarti, The Scared Books of The Jains, vol.5,p.5

[20] R.M.Das,op.cit,p.153

[21] R.M.Das,op,cit,p.154

[22] Heerala Jain, Bharateeya Samskarathinu Jainamathathinte Sambhavana,p.39

[23] E.V.Narayana Ayyar, Origin and Early History of Saivism in South India,p.147

[24] Heeralal Jain, op.cit,p.42

[25] Thomas Watters, On Yuvan Chveng's Travels in India,p.11

[26] Vincent A.Smith, The Oxford History of India, (e.d,) Percival Spear, p.79

[27] P.Thomas,op,cit.,p.75

[28] Augusta Klein, Legends and Myth of Spiritual India,p.262

[29] Heeralal Jain, op.cit,p.61

[30] Ibid.p.61

[31] Ibid,p.61

[32] Ibid,p.84

[33] Ibid,p.187

[34] Ibid,p.87

[35] G.jawaharlal, Jainism in Andhra,p.125

[36] P.Thomas, Hindu religion...op.cit,p.49

[37] Encyclopaedia Britannica, vol.II,p.869

CHAPTER TWO

EMERGENCE OF JAINISM IN KERALA

Kerala, the landscape spreading of Western Ghats, it has unique positions in geographically, cutting itself away from the mainstream Political history of the sub continents, it created a own identity in cultural, economic and social, the western part of the land is stretching towards 360 miles, situated between 8° 18' and 12° 48 North latitude and between 74°52' and 77° 24' longitude. Western Ghats act as the connecting link to the main land. Kerala made a remarkable identity of its own due to its geographical uniqueness and cultural specificity.

The geographical land of Kerala divided into three divisions such as, the high land, the mid land and the low land. The high land was covered by eastern border of Western Ghats, which has thick forest in upper ranges and lower ranges the forests are interested with Plantations. The western side of region was the land stretches along the coastal plain, the soil of the region is sandy, it suited for cultivation of coconut trees (Kalpa vriksha), which dominates the landscape and Paddy also cultivated here; Sand-witched between the low land and the high land is the mid land.

The land of Kerala soil is lateritic, it suitable for agricultural products such as, paddy, tapioca, spices and cashew being the most important crops. Tea and cardamom planted in higher elevation of land and in lower elevation, pepper, rubber, ginger and turmeric used to produce. Kerala is a separate territorial entity because of its geographical position from rest of India and being separated by Western Ghats, but not isolated from main stream of other part of the continents. The process of Aryanisation and origin and development of historical religion in other parts of India made their influence in the people of Kerala and its social structures. But the spread of classical cultural and process sanskritisation not reflect in Kerala due to isolation of the land. Before the Christian era the emissaries of Indo- Aryan began in Deccan.[1]

HISTORY OF JAINISM IN KERALA

Kerala was under the rule of many petty chieftains, especially Chera country, but not present day Kerala parts. Even though it extensive in the Coimbatore area of Tamil Nadu, so it might have been treated as part of Tamilagham, and it ruled by strong dynasty, when Jainism made its arrival in South India.

Accordingly the inscriptional evidence, Jainism flourished both Northern and Southern parts of Kerala. By the South, Kanyakumari may came under both Tamil Nadu and Kerala. The another position that North part of Kerala covered by Srvana-bel-gola and Jains took route of Cannanore of Malabar to Kodagu which denoted by Both folk literature of Malayalam and Kodagu. There are Kanada inscription in the Edakkal caves of Wynadu, so Jainism found in the north of Kerala which afiliations with Karnataka.

The Chera king Perum-Chera died by sat and facing North (Vadakkiruttal) which is similar to the practice of Jains namely Sallekhana and some of Chera genealogy has Jains, such as Ilango, the younger brother of the Chera King Chenkuttuvan of Silapathikaram who renounced the world at Kunavayil.

During 5th century Kunavayil was one of the famous Jain centre and this temple is mentioned in few inscriptions, which are discovered from Malabar and even 14th century Kavyas (Literature) also mentioned about this Jaina centre. But many of the Jaina temples were converted into Hindu temple even Kunavayil.

The Jaina monk refered as the word 'catukkal', which denoted in inscription of Kerala, it gave information that Jain monks enjoyed high prestige in the society.[2]

The people of Ancient Kerala welcomed both Indian and foreign religions along with philosophical ideas and system, which developed the cosmopoliten culture. People of Kerala followed primitive religions rites and practices. According to A.Sreedhara Menon, "The people, however, were so catholic in their outlook that they had no objection to worshipping in Jain or Buddhist shrines and performing vedic sacrifices, at the same time, both the influence of various religion and fundamental catholicity people were responsible for the making of cosmopolitan culture in Kerala".[3]

Tracing the impact of Jainism in Kerala was lapsed by the lack of details. But with the help of some of the Chera potentates were votaries of Jainism who scrupulously adhered to Jain rituals. Sangam Literature cities the Chera king Perumcheral bearing the tile of Atan, which denoting a Jain monk in the Prakrit form of Sanskrit Arhat[4] Perumcheral renounced the world by sitting to facing north by the guidance of Jain- the sallekhnavrata, it mentioned as 'vadakkirutal' in sangam literature[5] the endowment of Ilamkadungo to Jain ascetics mentioned in Pugalur inscription[6]. Jain influence was confirmed by Tirumalai Inscription of North Arcot district. It has the record of decadent of statues of Yaksha and Yakshi originally installed on the holy hill of Adigaman Elini of Chera Vamsathu (the chera dynasty) by Vidukkalakiya Perumal, the son of Raja Raja and a later descendant of Elini.[7] Elini mentioned as Keralabhuthra in sanskrit version of inscription and the Adigamans were deemed as kinsmen of Chera rulers. Ilamko Adigal, member of the Chera royalty and author of Silappathikaram also resided at Kunavayil Kottam, it was considered as Adiyakkunallur was Arukankoyil- which was a renowned place of Jain worship[8]

The Jain missionaries chose different centers in different parts for their religious activities, like Mysore and Tamil Nadu through these places they made their foot print in Kerala, but the lack of literary, epigraphical and archaeological evidence, couldn't trace their early achievements in this region. But their achievable actives of 9th and 11th centuries are available in different parts of Kerala. Among the rulers, the Chalukyas and Pallavas were encouraged rock –cut architecture; they experimented with the rock-cut and structural shrines, which were adopted and incorporated by Jains in Kerala. Both the Brahmanical and Jain sects adopted the same ritual services of the deities in newly constructed temples; even they had ideological and doctrinal differences.

Wyanad, one the famous regions in Kerala and also the centre of Jainas, few decades ago, the entire regions was covered by thick forest which as a shelter of wild animals alone, but it was cleared for cultivation, during that time some of the Jain monuments came to light. An un-noticed Vattezhuthu inscription was found near to the Jain Basti at Talakavu in Putadi village of South Wyanad found by Dr.K.K.N.Kurupu on 1970.[9] According to the Tirukkunavay Tevar's one hundred and thirty seven's texts, the Nalpattebbayiravar founded a Nakkaram and instituted a lamp and set apart some lands for the purpose.[10] The basis of characteristic of the script and style, Dr.M.G.S.Narayanan, approximately assigned its date of this inscription, which belonged to 9th century.[11] It highlights the foundation of a Tirukkuvanay Jain temple somewhere in the beginning of the 8th century CE[12]. The people of this region used this ruined Jain Basti as temple for Bagavathi worship, even the centre of trade also demolished and turned into forest land, which created problem to recover the history of Jainism in Kerala; Another Hindu temple of with huge deity of Ganapati, in its sanctum sanctorum in the area of Sultan Battery, which was a formerly a Jain Basti at Ganapati-Vattam.[13] Most of the Jain Basti in these regions was convereted into Hindu temples in due course when Hindu religion become strong and played a major force. There is no possible to assert to mention that, conversion of Jain Basti into Hindu temple by the support of ruler or may be the willingness of devotees with natural process. In many other places in Wyanad, such as, Arepati, Vennayod, Palakkunnu, Manantod and Varatur Jain Monuments of later period can be found.[14]

The Department of History, Calicut University has discovered an ancient Jain Basti at Talakkavu near Putadi in Wyanad. The inscription of Muttuaimappatteshu(one hundred and fifty seventh year) indicate about the date of erection of Jain Vihara and this lead to founding of the vihara at the beginning of the 8th century of the Christian era.[15]

Another inscription from Kinalur, near Balusseri published as no.14 of 1901, which has the name of the Chera King Vijayaraja, till to found its unknown to the Kerala historians, who shown as a patron of Jainism and devote of Tirukkunavay.[16] On 1970 this region was excavated by Archaeological survey of India, which revealed a portion of a medieval citadel and the foundation of medieval temple of peculiar shape belonged to 8th or 9th century, by the light of Putadi-Talakkavu inscriptions, these remnants may be identified as belonging to the old Tirukkunavay shrine. During the incursions of Tippu Sultan period, Jain population nearly 2,000 migrants from Mysore and settled in Kalpetta. Some other Jain influence centres were Varatur, Vennayottu and Palakkunnu; still Jains managed two temples in Puttananati, which has both Jain and Hindu gods and goddesses for worship.

Jain monuments studded with hills can see in Tiruchchanattumalai near Chitaral which is erstwhile Vilavangode taluk of Travancore. Cavern temple of Bagavathi with icons was identified with that of Ambika yakshi, Parsavanatha, Mahavira and other Tirthankaras. The Ay king Vikramaditya Varaguna was a Hindu though; he had endowed this temple on 925 CE. This place is well famous in earlier times, so it attract Jains from other places like Tirunanrungondai in Tirukkoyilur taluk of the South Arcot district, Kudavasal in the Tanjore district etc. the inscription in archaic Vattezhuthu script, which mentioned the names and other details etc... of the persons who carved them under the seat of the votive figures.

The Kinalur near Balusseri inscription of Vattezhuthu gave evidence for the prominence to Tirukkunavay in

Kerala, which deals about the institution of rice-offerings and permanent lamp to the palli of Vijayarageeswaram at Kunavaynallurthi.[17] This proves that, Jainism was patronised by this ruler and this place was one of the activate centers of Jains in Malabar. It is supposed that the palli was established by the Chera King Vijayaraja who must be attributed to the close of 9th century CE.[18]

Trikkannamatilakam, near Cragannore went under archaeological excavation, it revealed out the foundation of a medieval temple of a peculiar shape belonging to the 8th or 9th century.[19] The believed that these relics belonged to the temple and monastery of Jains of the famous Kunavayir Kottam in Kerala. The literary evidence of 14th and 15th centuries indicates Trikkannamathilakam, known as Tirukkunavay also was in a prosperous status. Some of the places exposed Jain monuments, like, Manjeswar, Kallil near Perumbavoor, Jainamedu near Palakkad and Chitral (Cape Comerin district), the availability of monuments in these places enhance the fact that the Jaina activities and Cultural legacy of a by-gone age in Kerala. The icons of Tirthankaras, Yaksha and Yakshis found in these places, contribute a significant chapter to the history of art, sculpture and iconography of Kerala.[20]

Even now good numbers of Jain followers are residing in Wyanad. Most of them belonged to Digambara sect and they are identified with the term Goundas. Both Parsvanatha and Mahavira are more popular deities among them. This part of Kerala, continuing the cultural legacy, and community of Jain form 9th century CE without any interruption. The migration of Jains came from Sravana Balgola, important Jain centre, in the South. But by the influence of Hinduism, Jains lost their identity and completely wiped off from other part of Kerala. Culturally and topographically, Wyanad, the frontier part of ancient Kerala, related with Karnataka, where Jainism had strong position in significant political and social force in the annals of history. The remaining parts of Kerala had been largy influenced by the Bhakti movement of Tamilnadu under the Alvars and Nayanmars.[21]

The influx of Vaishnavism was created by the common identity and assimilation among the devotees of Vishnu and Parsvanatha. The cultural history of Kerala was clearly explained about the spread of Vaishnavism. The Nagaraja Temple of Nagarcoil, a Jain centre of worship, which formerly included in the kingdom of Travancore.[22] The donation was given to this Jain shrine by Venad ruler, Bhutala Veera Udaya Marthana Varma, the ruler of Venad on 1521 CE.[23] The shrine Kamala Vahana Pandita and Guna Veera Pandita were accepted the association of Jain priests. The Jain icons of the temple were now treated as that of Hindu Gods. The hooded serpent which provided the umbrella for Parsavanatha deity is now worshipped as the great serpent Ananta of Vishnu. This was a significant change, almost equal to self-negation for Jainism.

Jains had left Kerala and its significant legacy from north to south and east to west like the followers of Hindu religion in the contemporary period. The rules and regulation of Tirumulikkalam temple located in near to the Chera capital Makotai as model or precedent to be followed by other temples of Kerala. The same manner, the temple of Tirukkunavay situated in Tirukannamatilakam had been a model for many of Jain Bastis in Kerala.[24] The yard of Tirukkunavay deity had also been cited in a few inscriptions. Those who violated these regulations prescribe for Jain temple was considered as an offence against the deity of Tirukkunavay.

There was a constant and strong competition between the Jains and the Brahmanical people regarding the construction and increase the number of temple in Kerala as elsewhere in India. Shift from vanavasa or settled life in monasteries was emphasised by medieval Jainism. The Varanagacarita clearly recommends that, Jain temple must be built to maintain the unimpaired existence of the Jain religion.[25] It was also stated that the construction of Jain temples for a person engrossed in worldly affairs to attain heaven. Same rituals and practices followed in both Jains and Brahmins temples in Kerala, which were instituted for devotees. The rituals of Brahmins such as the rice-offering, Nanda Vilakku or permanent lamp, Sribali, Santi, Kuta(Umbrella), and Candanam(sandlepaste) were such items found in Jain temples also.

Silappathikaram written by Ilango Adikal, one of the great classics of India and a general education based book of Karma and its reactions was the main inspiration of Jain religion. This classical poem consists of all sorts of information, history merging into myth, caste customs, and spread of Brahmanism, religious rites, military lore and description of city and country life. The classical and folk of cultural current were awarded by the author, so he integrate those current of folk religion with the religion of the sophisticated people.[26] His message to all the inhabitants is: “Seek God and serve those who are near him, Do not tell lies, Avoid slander, Avoid eating the flesh of animals, Do not cause pain to any living things, Be charitable, and observe fast days, Never forget the good others have done to you. Avoid bad company, Never give false evidence, Do not disguise the truth, Stay near those who fear God..., The days of your life are numbered, You cannot escape from your fate. Seek the help of everything that leads you to the ultimate goal in life."[27] The message of Illango Adikal was based on Mahaveera's ideals, it highly provide foundation for the universal religion and fraternity of humanity.

The ideals of Jainism are close resemblance with Buddhism and its organization made some of the former bequeath a common cultural legacy also a significant contribution. In Kerala, the propagation of non-violence preached by both Jain as well as Buddhist monks, Most of the blood-rites of animals were left off by those practitioners. So they practised the rite of 'Gurusi' made out of the Chunam (lime) and turmeric was used as substitude for blood-rites in the temple of Bhagavati and Teyyattam. The Tamil word Kuruti means blood offered by Velan in his auspicious Kalam which it turned into Gurusi as a sanskritised, by the impact of Jainism, this is a significant cultural change in the rituals of Kerala.[28]

Improve the growth of knowledge; Jains gave land as gift by the practice of four-fold gifts of shelter, food, medicine and knowledge and emphazised these principles as the highest forms of piety. Later days most of the Brahmanical temples of Kerala were followed this customs, for the spread of education, Jain monasteries played a tremendous role. The school is known by the term "pallikudam" in Malayalam language, which connotes the relationship between the earliest centres of education with the non-vedic centres known by the term "palli"[29]The Jain monastery gave shelter to both homeless and their teachers imparted education. Jains not only in cult the education, even though, they practiced medicine out of mere charity. The Jvalini Kalpa, treaties from Jaina Tantra, prepared by the Jains in Mysore, suggests the monks functioned as physicians and used indigenous herbal for medicine.[30]

The ensurement of Jains influence in Kerala could be seen in the induction of Jain terminology in Malayalam. The earliest votaries of Dravidian literature appear to have been Jains. Robert Caldwell most pertinently remarks, “Doubtless the Jains themselves used Sanskrit in southern as in northern India at the commencement of their work as teachers before they set themselves to the task of developing amongst each of the Dravidian races a popular literature independent of their rivals the Brahmins”. The Jains stand against the spread of Sanskrit by an anti brahminical feelings in the old Pandya country and undertook the writing of grammatical and rhetorical works.

The Tantric cult became a significant force in early medieval period, it made disappear some of the traditions in Kerala. Kumari Puja –the cult of maidens, which included the worship of unmarried teenaged and underaged girls, was a part of Tantric cult. The Jaina text of ‘Bhairava Padmavadi Kalpa’ written by Mallisena Sari also mentioned about this cult. The worship, treated girls as manifestation of Sakthi. ‘Silappatikaram’- the Tamil epic indicated guardin goddess of Aiyai, a virgin girl of the Einar.[31] They adorned a maiden of their tribe as Aiyai and placed before her, the offerings of cooked rice, spices and flesh, and she took for procession to their temple. This cult is probably a non-brahmanical and aboriginal in origin. This cult influence the Jains also, the ‘Bairava Padmavati Kalpa’- the Jain treatise, denoted that the worshipper chose two, seven year old girls. The previous night of the day of worship they gave only milk to those girls, and provided grass bed for sleep during night and in the morning, they are to be bathed and clad in white clothes.[32] It also a system that, the girls should be offered what they wanted to eat. On each occasion of worship of these girls they were to be provided with four dishes, sixteen arecanuts and thirty two betel leaves.[33] Whatever origin of this cult the Jains had also adopted this cult as a religious rites. The Jains had their own contribution in the legacy of the cult of 'Talappoli' in shrine and Bhagavathi temples of Kerala, and 'Teyyattam' of Bhagavathi is performed in the shrines of Kavus of north Malabar, where the practice of virgin worship observed in festivals. The virigin girls who had observed several rituals like holy bath and clad in white clothes proceed with 'Talappoli' before the Teyyam of Bhagavathi. The eight auspicious articles like umbrella, conch, swastika, purana kumbha and mirror are provided for prosperity and happiness during the time of festival and other occasions, this custom also relating to Jainism.[34]

In non-brahminical centre of worship like 'Kavus' and 'kottams' and 'velichappatan' still observe Mundanam' or full-shaving of their heads as a religious custom which is derived from the practice of Jain and Buddhist monks. They have also to observe strict vegetarianism. These rituals are greatly influenced by the 'sramanik' concepts of Jainism and Buddhism. The cults of Serpent, Yaksha, Yakshi had a significant place in Jainism. The folk life and religion of Kerala had been largely influenced by these cults. The snake worship of 'kulams' and 'Naga Yakshi' concepts have a cultural relation with primitive religion and Jainism.

However the impact of Jainism on the religious life of Kerala had been found meager by scholars. William Logan, in his, Malabar Mannual, is of the opinion that: "Jainism seems to have made very little impression on the religious belief of the people, for even a regard for animal life, the great characteristic of the Jains, had until recent years, very little hold on the people, and even now the great bulk of the Hindu population feed on fish and flesh when they can get it, and it is only the unenlightened upper classes, who are under the Brahminical influence, who observe the practice of abstaining from flesh".[35]

The contribution to the cultural heritage of Kerala was esteem by Jains and both historical relics and monuments of Jainism still exist in various parts of Kerala. Wyanand and Manjesher has uninterrupted continuity of the Jain community, they still living these areas and not wiped off as like as Buddhism from Kerala. Jains lost their goals and separate cultural identity in Kerala by adopted several Brahminical rituals and the process of Aryanisation.

References

[1] V.A.Smith, The Oxford History of India,p.42

[2] P.K.Gopalakrishnan, Jainamatam Keralattil, The Government of Kerala, Thiruvananthapuram,1974,pp.12-35

[3] Ibid

[4] P.K.Gopalakrishnan, Janmitham Keralathil,p.3

[5] Ibid,p.115

[6] K,A.Neelakanda Sastri, A History of South India,op.cit.p.70

[7] South Indian inscriptions, Vol.V.No.784.p.338

[8] P.N.Elamkulam Kunjan Pillai, Keralacharithrathinte Eruladanja Edukal, pp.95-106

[9] Quoted M.G.S.Narayanan, "New Light on Kunavayir Kottam and the Date of Cilappathikaram", Journal of Indian History, XLVIII, part III, p.694

[10] Ibid,p.694

[11] Ibid,p.701

[12] Ibid,p.694

[13] K.K.Ramachandran Nair, Gazetteer of India, Kerala state Gazetteer, Vol.II,Part II,p.230

[14] K.K.N.Kurupu, Aspects of Kerala History and Culture,p.2

[15] M.G.S.Narayanan, Re-Interpretations in South Indian History,pp,69-70

[16] Ibid,p.73

[17] M.R.Raghavavarier, Keraleeyatha – Charithramanagal,p.79

[18] M.G.S.Narayanan, New Light on Kunavayir Kottam and the Date of Cilappatikaram, p.695

[19] B.B.Lal, Indian Archaeology – A Review,pp.13-15

[20] Stella Kramrisch, The Art and Crafts of Kerala,pp.70-71

[21] R.G.Bhandarkar, Vaishnavism, Saivism and Minor Religious systems, pp.48-50

[22] T.A.Gopinatha Rao, Travancore Archaeological Series Vol. II, Part.II, p.127

[23] Ibid,p.128

[24] T.K.Krishna Menon, "Malabar Temples" Bulletin of the Ramavarma Research Institute, Vol.V, Part II, p.15

[25] Nath Nandi, Religious Institutions and Cults in the Deccan, p.13

[26] N.Vanamamalai, Studies in Tamil Literature, p.47

[27] Illango Adikal, 'Silappatikaram' Trans., Alain Danielou, pp.202-203

[28] Ibid

[29] M.R.Raghavavarier, Ammavazhi Keralam, Kerala Sahitya Academy, p.133

[30] Ramendra Nath Nandi, Religious Institution and Cults in the Deccan,p.105

[31] Illango Adikal, Silappathikaram,pp,76-77, Vanamamalai, Studies on Tamil Literature.p.22

[32] Ramendra Nath Nandi.,op.cit,p.22

[33] Ibid.p.125

[34] T.A. Gopinatha Rao, Travancore Archaeological Series, p.127.

[35] William Logan, Malabar Mannual, Vol.I, p.185

CHAPTER THREE

JAINISM AND JAIN TEMPLES IN PALAKKAD

Kerala emerged as a homogeneous political state of the Indian Union on 1st November 1956. During the time of India independence in 1947, Kerala remained as three distinct political sections, namely British Malabar as part of the Madras presidency and the Princely states of Cochin and Travancore. While Malabar was under the direct rule of the British power on 1st January 1957, Malabar district was trifurcate into three districts, viz., Cannore, Kozhikode and Palakkad. The Palakkad district thus formed consists of old Valluvand Taluk, Palghat Taluk and a portion a Ponnani Taluk of Malabar district and Chittur Taluk of the erstwhile Travancore-Cochin state. S.C.Batt denoted that, "Palakkad lies between North latitude 10 degree 20' and 11 degree 14' and east longtitude 76 degree 20' and 76 degree 54'. Palakkad district is bound by Nilagiri district on the North, Coimbatore district on the west."[1]

JAIN CENTRES IN KERALA

In Kerala, period between 2nd century AD to 6th or 7th century AD as era of spread of Jainism, it proved by inscriptional evidence, but at the same time no single inscription found out in the territories of Kerala related about the span of Jainism. The state re-organisation act of 1957 only made Kanyakumari as part of Tamil Nadu, before years it was integral part of Kerala, especially Travancore state and the avent of Jainism in this area in 9th century AD only, so it gave conclusion that Jainism rose in Kerala later than 9th century AD. Even though it suffered a lot in the hands of some set of Hinduism and Jain temple converted into Hindu temple; Jain communities are found in some parts of Kerala such as Wynadu and Kassaragod and Vestiges of Jain can see in Palakkadu, Thrissur and Eranakulam districts.

Calicut District:

Svetambara set of Jain temple found in near the railway station of Calicut with recent constriction of under the control of Gujaraties of that city.

Eranakulam District:

In Erunakulam district, Jain temple can found in two places such as, Kallil and Tirukkumavay

Kallil:

Perumbavur in Kallil has rock-cut Jain temple with deity, Bhagavati, might been a Jaina Yaksi in the beginning, some other attraction with that is rock cut icons and unfinished Mahavira, this is only cave temple for proving the Jain vestiges in Kerala which is worshipped by people of Kochi and nearest area of Ernakulam

Tirukkunavay:

The Present Trikkana-matilakam which is ancient Tirukkunavay, Ilango, the author of Silapathikaram, stayed in Kunavay, which situated 13 Km away from Kodungallur (Cranganore), Tirunannur inscription mentioned same temple and character of Vatteluttu denoted the practices of grant of Tirukkunavay, along with this, one more inscription from Alattur, also indicated about same area temple, and it strengthen by Malayalam (Literature) poetic works of 14th century AD. Eminent scholars like M.G.S. Narayanan, strongly denoted that Tirukkunavay was Jaina establishment from the 8th & 9th centuries AD and more than couple of centuries.[2]

Kassaragod District:

The District of Kassaragod has two Jain temples; one is a ruined condition and another located in Southern Bank of the river in Bangara Manjesvara and Chaturmukka respectively. The temple of Bangara Manjesvara has the icons like Adi-natha, Santi-natha, Canda-natha and Vardhamana are in sanctum, the age of temple is three centuries old and it renovated recently. The temple of Chatur Mukha also located in same district. It has both metal images and icons, such as caubisi (24 Tirthankaras in one) especially Parsvanatha in Kayotsarga position and remaining like Kusmandini, Padmavati and Sarasvati in icons forms. Suparsvanatha is one of the beautiful image of this temple is made up of alloys. The basadi in desolate condition, so it may be very old one compared with other temples.

Palakkadu District:

Alattur, IssaranKodu, Jainamedu and Pallikikulam parambu are four Jain centres in Palakkadu District

Alattur:

The image Mahavira, in Paryankasana pose revealed from this place along with lion cognizance and the triple umbrella are seen. Gandharavas flank in both side with holding fly wisk and akimbo in both right and left sides respectively. One more icon Parsavanatha standing in Kayotsarga posture under canopy of three hoods. An inscription with ancient script denoted about palli of this place and Tirukkunavay.

Issaran-kodu:

Issaran Kodu is situated in 18Km away from Main place of Palakkadu. In this temple, the idols of Parsavanatha and Mahavira were installed and worship is conducted. Once upon a time it was a great centre of Jainism but it changed in due course of time due to invasion. Along with Issaran Kodu and another two places were occupied by Jains in course of time, such as, Varuvesseri and Cuvanna-Mannu Jaina inscription has been recorded from Talakkavu.

Jainamedu:

There is a Jain temple with the deity of Chandranatha, located on the bank of the river Kalppatti river in the village of Cadakkettara, this ruined temple renovated in 1967, and another deities are, Yakshis, Vijaya, Padmavati and Jvalamalini along with idols of Parsvanatha and Rishaba deva, this place is called as Jainamedu which means the hills of the Jainas. In early period another two more Jain temple were presented. One of the well-known family of Jainamedu, constructed and maintained one Vidyalaya, for imparting both religious and secular knowledge to students.

Palliikkulam-Parambu:

The idols of Parsavanatha and Mahavira were found in the village of Kavasseri of Pallikkulam-Parambu with an inscription, belonged to 10th century A.D. This place was a Jain centre, it proved by incomplete inscription.

Tirukkur:

This place has cave temple, currently under the control of the Hindus, some of them mentioned that, the cave temple belonged to Jaina, A.Sreedhara Menon, denoted that Iru-nilam- kodu also one of the Jain temple.

Thrissur District

There is no strong evidence that Thrissur, is one of the Jain centre, but this place has famous Hindu temple of Koodal-Manikyam of Irinjalakkuda, with presiding deity of Bharata, which they considered it as Jain temple previously.[3]

The name Palghat has different versions and it derived from the Traditional Tamil Classification of land on the basis of social formations and physical features. Palghat can never come under the traditional classification of pala region by analysis with the fertile plains of the district and other physical features of the place.[4]

The one more arguments is based on the Jaina tradition about Palghat, that the Jains came and settled in this place, which turned into Jainamedu in later days, the argument is that, the Jains speak Pali language, and they occupied this area, so it called as Palighat and later it transformed into Palaghat. By the work of Dr.Francis Bachanan, A Journey from Madras through the Countries of Mysore Canara and Malabar, he repeatedly refers to Palighat.[5] Apart from this, one more apt argument is that the whole of Palghat and its suburbs were once covered by thick forests of Pala (Alsteria Scholaris) trees; so the words Pala + Kadu came to be known as Palakkad or Palghat.[6]

During the period between the 9th /10th centuries and the 16th century CE, the Jainism had glory and established a network of Jaina centres.[7] Some of these are located in Palakkad. The four major centres of Jainism scattered in and around Palakkad are namely Paruvassery Palli, Chakkyarthotam in Kavassery, Eswarankod in Mundur and Jainamedu in Palakkad.

Palakkad becoming one of the oldest centres of Janinsm in Kerala due to various reasons, Jains entered into Kerala by two ways such as, by Karnataka to Palghat and the bordering of Thiruvanathapuram attracted Jainas from Tamil Nadu. Jainas came to Palakkad through the Kongu regions with which the region had a longstanding cultural contact. Tamil Nadu and the northern and southern parts of Kerala such as Kozhikode, Ponnani and Kodungallur were linked by the gap of Palghat.

Jainism had stronghold in Tamil Nadu districts, such as, Kanchi, Ponnur, Cittamur, Pudukkottai, Madurai and Tinnevelly. The Kongu kings (Ratta/Ganga Kings) were devout Jains.[8] P.B. Desai denoted that, the earliest Jaina monuments in Tamil Nadu could be traced back to as early as the second century BCE[9]and it had suffered a temporary setback during 7th century in Tamil Nadu.[10] By the influence of Pallava, they ruined the architectures and the Jains entered Palakkad. There are evidences to establish that the Kongu region had influenced the developments in Palakkad. During the 9th century the Chola ruler invaded the Chittur from Kongu land considered as the historical traditions. Palakkad has earliest Jain momuments dated 10th -11th century. It proved that, the Palakkad had the Jain settlements were well established in 10th century CE. But there is no confimation about the settlements of Jains in Alathur Taluk.

Everyone face problem about the evolution of the history of Jainism in Palakkad due to the paucity of sources; and this is a common problem for whole state, while compared the hundreds of inscription available in the state of Karnataka for enable to make a better understanding of Jainismin those parts, but very less amount of inscriptions only available in Kerala. But in Wayanad has an only place for sufficient accounts of inscriptions for the trace of the details of settlements of Jains, but the information related to later period. The inscription of Edakkal cave of Sultan

Battery contains details of Kadambas (c.300-c.500CE), a connected account of Jainism in Kerala is impossible.

Jain shrines of early period has been located, few in number; while in Karnataka, the earliest Jain Basti is dated to the fifth century CE, Kerala's shrine are of a later period. By the archaeological proof, Palakkad is one of the sites where Jainism was in glorious status. According to P.K.Gopalakrishnan, Jaina faith had a wider appeal in Palakkad-Alathur reigon.[11]But there is doubt that Jainism had attained high level in the district, because the total population of Jains was very low in 20th century. Through the notes of C.A. Innes, there were thirty Jains living in Palakkas and Mundur.[12] The Census report of 1971 denoted that, Jain population shrank to twelve.[13]

The Jaina tradition, mentioned that the entry of Jainas in Palakkad, started from Mysore in the 15th century.[14] The four merchants – Ijjanna Sutter, Lakkappa Sutter, Doddapayappa Sutter and Chikupayappa Sutter- were immigrated from Kellampulli in Mysore to Palghat, to escape from persecution by the then Raja of Mysore.[15]This information proved that, Jainism came under severe strain in Karnata from 13th century onwards.[16] The Jainas settled down at Manikkapattanam and Muttupattanam after purchasing these lands from the Palakkad Raja.

According to the some of the tradition, There was no enormous size of number of Jains not came from Karnatak to Kerala especially in Wyanad, due to Hyder's and Tippu's attack on Jains. Jaina Monuments in Kerala divided into three categories:

1. Early structure converted into Hindu temples
2. Shrine found in ruined form in and around state

3. Temples, maintained by the existing Jaina population of Kasagod, Kozhikode, Wayanad, Palakkad, Eranakulam and Alappuzha.

The district of Palaghat has Jaina monumnets, but which converted into Hindu temple. The intensive study of Hindu temples only can prove these facts. The view of Researcher Ronald M. Bernier, many of these cave temple of Jainas and Jaina temple at Alathur, most associated with Bhagavathi temple in Palaghat by the extinct of architectural and sculptural features.[17] Some of the Jaina shrine that have been converted in to Hindu temple in Kerala, those are Chitharal (Bhagavathi), Kallil (Bhagavathi), Matilakam (Siva), Koodalmanikkam (Bharatha), Paruvasseri (Vishnu) and Tiruvannur (Siva).

The team of Archaeologist from the Department of Archaeology, Kerala University conducted a research about Jain Shrine at Godapuram in the Kavassery Panchayat of Alathur district on 1960. A Vattezhutu inscription found in Alathur, which denoted the information about that, the property of temple should protect by Arunuttuvar and if any misuse of property is considered to be offence against of Tirukkunavay Tevar. According to M.G.S. Narayanan indicate that it was a medium size temple of 10th -11th centuries A.D.[18]

The ruined Jain temple at Chakkyar thottam or Kundam on a hillock known as Pallikkunra noticed by The State department of Archaeology, Kerala on 1960.[19] The remaining parts of shrine such as beams, pillars and slabs are found in and around of the site Tiruchur Archaeologist Museum exhibited the sculptures of Mahaveera and Parsvanatha and fragmentary of Vattezhuthu inscription of these shrine.[20]

The image of Mahaveera seated in Paryankasana poses with triple umbrella, nudity, the lanchana of two lions and chauri bearing gandharvas and another thirthankara Parsavanatha stand in Kayotsarga pose under canopy of three serpent hoods.[21] Some of the part of shrine such as beams, pillars and slabs are found the site. Alathur-ruined shrine is one among the four oldest Jaina structural shrines which is the model of Matilakam shrine, remaining shrine are found at Thalakkavu in Wayanad and Kinalur in Kozhikode respectively.

There are many more ruined stone-built shrines are found in the vicinity of Alathur. Ruins of a granite temple found in Kallamparambu (land of stones). Most of part in scattered but only adisthana of the temple in good shape, but the local people of this place, installed a picture of Kali and started worshipping it. Later years, local people collected the scattered stones and formed a circle around a banyan tree standing on one side of the compound. A well is also found nearby.

Paryankasana pose of Mahavira is graceful and the proportion are well modeled the face displays inner composure and self-absorption with round and ears are long and stented. It has Straight and square shoulders with beautifully modeled arms and body.

The Jain sculpture has triple umbrella, nudity, long arms, youthful body and the lanchana of Mahavira, namely the lions, but usual mark of Jain Sculpture are absent. The right hand side of statue, the Gandharvas hold the cauris and in left hand side hold akimbo, and the side of Mahavira, carved with two lions with palm.

The second sculpture parsvanatha has cracks here and there but all lanchanas for the Jain figure are not seen in the sculpture and one and only a three-headed cobra alone is seen instead of seven or five headed cobra above parsavanatha. The hand and body indicate deep meditation, with round face and truck is nude. Some of the Jaina figures, like Srivatsa Symbol, Yaksha figures, Yaksha Dharamendra and Yakshini Padmavati are absent. [22]

Chimbachala is another ruined Temple found around Alathur, the appearance of temple like Architectural features and sculptural representations on the panels of the Adisthana looks Jaina shrine along with that one small shrine located to left side of sanctum of large temple, may be it have been the earliest rock-cut shrines built in Kerala. It built of rectrangular stones and roofing is in vaulting technique without the use of morator or plaster, the features of temple depicted 9th century sculpture. It is a greater possibility of these structures being once Jaina shrine at Godapuram. The Survey of Alathur-Bhagavati and Shiva shrine would help to identify the Jaina temple.

Paruvassery Hindu temple as Palliyara Bhagavathi Temple is famous one, compared with Jain temple. According to Raghava Variyar, "A scrutiny of the idols reveals that it is a Jaina temple, and Jwalamalini, the Yakshi of Chandraprabha Thirthankara located in sanctum sanctorial and idol of Thirthankara himself can be seen next to it. An inscription found at the base of idol, which is now worshiped as Shasthavu". [23]

According to the tradition, There are only two Jaina Bastis existed in Palaghat, one at Manikkapattanam known as Doddai Basti and another one is Chikka-Basti, at Muttapattanam which one associated with Hyder and Tippu destruction process of temple. Rishabha Thirthankara temple at Muttapattanam completely destroyed by Tippu and its granite slabs used for the construction of the fort.[24] Land of Jain passed to the hand of the local Tamil Brahmins.

Most of the Tamil bramins were employed by both Hyder Ali and Tipu Sultan in their service during Mysorean occupation[25] and the Kalpathy Viswanatha Swami Temple Devaswam hold the land of Jain which was confiscated from Mattupattanam. Now, the only remnant of the shrine at Muttapattanam is a Balipitha. Even Mr.Innes also denoted that, only one or two stones are now visible,[26] and during 1939, V.C. Vijayachandra a Jain wrote about this Balipitha which found at Muttupattanam with the images of Nagas that might be originally part of the basti in ruins.[27]

The one more Jaina shrine of Eswaran in ruined form found at Velikkadu in Mundur, nearly fifteen km from Palghat. The Eswara Kota names come from family of Eswaran Kdadam who stayed near to this temple. From the ruined temple the images of Mahaveera and Parsvanatha found in plot owened by a person named Divakaran.[28]

M.R. Raghava Variyar denoted that, idol from Eswaran Kota, is distinguished from other idols, those are in Kerala and it has unique position, the idol look like, in deep meditation in Paryankasana beneath a tree, it not represent any other Thirthankara.[29] Another Expert P.B.Desai points that, the idols are renamed as Pindi Kadavul, the name Pindi stands for Ashoka tree; he noted out, chaitya of Mallinatha Thirthankara, is Pindi Kadavul which stand for Thirthankara himself.[30]

Jainamedu, known as Manikkapattanam, has Jain shrine which is the only shrine maintained by Jains.[31] According to tradition, origin of the name of Manikkapattanam, is one Manikam, included in the thousand putiyapanams given to king for purchasing of land for settlement of Jains, the settlement located on the

Southern bank of Kalpathi river, it extended upto Vadakanthara.[32]The Agarasala of the temple at Manikkapattanam was set fire and around the wall of granite parapet was demolished, the shrine's main deity, the idol of Chandranatha, was also mutilated. [33]

The temple of Manikkapattanam is small rectangular building, 32 ft by 20 ft fully covered by granite. The roof is terraced type with granite beams and second tiled had roof, ruined mantapam or a raised floor in front in the temple.[34] The main building northern cornor had circular stone well, and inside the shrine, there are four chambers; the first chamber had chandranatha shrine in white marble, and around it is a passage through, where man can freely walk. The image of Vijayaksha and Jwalamalinidevi in second chamber and images of Rishabha Thirthankara, Parsvanatha, Siddhar and Gumata Raja, Dharanendra Padmavati and Brahma Yaksha in third chamber. The Worshipped Nagas, which is located in left side of idols, and the fourth chamber, is vacant without any images. The Jaigandy or gong is hung is hung there for being rug at the time of worship, and the compound with stone image of Kshetrapala.[35] The medieval period, sculptures are found in this shrine but could not trace exact date of construction of this shrine due to it renovated and rebuilt many times. Jainas of Mundur restored one small rectangular building of stone which denoted by Researcher Innes.[36] The image of old temple can found by Characteristic of the medieval shrines even it renovated in 1962.[37]

According to the view of scholars, which some more structure might connect to Jainism in Palghat. Specially, Velayuden Panikassery denoted that, Mannarghat, Pallikkurup, Thachmbara, Nattukallu and Thuppanat are some of the sites association with Jainism.[38] A.Sreedhara Menon, denoted that, both temples at Irunilakod and Tirukkur were also Jaina shrines.[39]

Since, there is no deep and keen studies have been attempted to study about the distinctive features of architectural and sculptural characteristics of the Jaina or Buddhist temple and Hindu temples of the period between 9th century AD to 16th century AD. Archaeologist excavation conducted in Alathur and Jainamedu some of the ruined structure were found which converted to Hindu temple that experts of architectural and sculptural styles clearly identified as Jaina.

Finally, compared with various Jaina temples in Palghat, the one and only temple at Jainamedu is still surviving in all its glory, rest of other temples either on the verge of ruin or has been converted to Hindu temples. Some of the questions decrease the popularity of Jainamedu that Jainas handed over temple to trust and planned to return back to Karnataka, their native land.

References

[1] S.C.Batt, The Encyclopaedic District Gazateers of India South Zone, Vol II, p.1

[2] M.G.S. Narayanan, Kunavyil Kottam in Cultural symbiosis in Kerala History Association, 1972; A Sreedhara Menon, A Survey of Kerala History, (S.P.C.S) Kottaayam, Kerala , 1970. P.89

[3] A.Sreedhara Menon, A survey of Kerala History, (S.P.C.S) Kottayam, Kerala, 1970,p.89

[4] C.K.Kareem, Kerala District Gazatters-Palakkad, p.1

[5] A.A.Malayali, Palakkad District Directory, 1994,p.1; Palakkad Directory, 1986,p.28

[6] C.K.Kareem, op,cit,p.1; Palakkad Director,p.28

[7] Ronald M Bernier, Temple Arts of Kerala,p.2

[8] P.K.Gopalakrishnan, Jainamatham...op.cit.,p.51

[9] P.B.Desai, op.cit,p.9

[10] Ibid.p.9

[11] P.K.Gopalakrishnan,op,cit,p.51

[12] C.A.Innes, Malabar Gazetteer,p.473

[13] Ibid,p.473

[14] Matruboomi,Malayalam News Paper, 17 December 2004

[15] V.C.Vijaya Chandra Jain, “The Jain Temple at Palghat”, p.205

[16] P.B.Desai,op.cit,p.401

[17] Ronald M. Bernire, op.cit,p.2

[18] M.G.S.Narayanan, Perumals of Kerala,p.184

[19] N.G.Unnithan, ‘Journal of Indian History’, Vol.XLVI, Part-II, “Relics of Jainism-Alathur”,pp.537-43

[20] M.G.S.Narayanan, Kunavayil Kottam...op,cit,p.540; Appedix A.

[21] N.G.Unnithan, op.cit,p.540

[22] N.G.Unnithan, op.cit,p.540

[23] M.R. Raghava Varier, Keraleeyatha Charithramanagal, p.76

[24] Mathurboomi, Malayalam News Paper, November 11, 2006

[25] C.K.Kareem, op.cit,p158

[26] C.A.Innes,op.cit,p.473

[27] V.C.Vijayachandra Jain, op.cit,p.206

[28] Personal Interview with Divakaran, October 13, 2007

[29] M.R. Raghava Varier, Smaskara Keralam, Malayalam quarterly, Vol.III, No.1, Govt of Kerala,p.49

[30] M.R.Raghavarier, Keraleeyatha....p.76

[31] Malayala Manorama, Malayalam News Paper,June 8, 2002.

[32] V.C.Vijaya Chandra Jain, op.cit,p.206

[33] Ibid,p.206

[34] Ibid,p.204

[35] Ibid,p.205

[36] C.A.Innes, op.cit, p.473

[37] M.R.Raghava Varier,op.cit,p.76

[38] Velayudan Panikasery, Kevala Charita Patanagal, Vol-I,p.166

[39] A.Sreedhara Menon, op.cit, p.89

CHAPTER FOUR

JAIN FESTIVALS

Indian culture, shaped by many causes and sect, one among that is Jainism. The Jain's the concept of Ahimsa (non-violence), Satya (Truthfulness), Acaurya (non-stealing), Brahmacharya (chastity), made strong foundation of Dharma and those who are followed this Jain principle by austere life. At the same time Jainism followed socio-religious harmony by the policy of 'give and take', through this attitude it accepted many features from other religion, even though it accepted good morals from Vedas.

Each and every culture has some festivals to represent their faith and differ from others. Jainism also have some of the festivals which are similar with Hindus but in different manner. 'Parvan' is general name for festival of Jainism.[1]

Nitya and Naimittika Parvas:

Generally Jain festivals divided in two types such as regular and occasional it terms as Nitya and Naimittika respectively. There are five Nitya parvas such as, Dvittya (Second lunar day), Pancami(fifth lunar day), Astami (eighth lunar day), Ekadasi (Elevanth lunar day) and Caturdasi (fourteenth lunar day), these five parvas are considered holy day by house holders and observe for austere practices.

Akshaya-Tritiya

This parva celebrate on third day of the bright fortnight of the month of Vaisakha, which means 'thirdday of unending prosperity'. The day, a Jaina saint Sreyamsa offering food to Adinath- the first Tirthankara who was fast for one year. This day Jain people offer sugar juice to Thirthankara and ablution with milk, sandal paste and tender coconut juice and the idol of the Jain taken for around the street, and people respect their,Thirthankara by liting lamps.

Ananta Chaurdasi

This festival is celebrated in honour of Ananthanatha, the 14th Tirthankara, charities are offered to the needy on this day and previous day of this day is spent in austerities fourteenth lunar day.

Ashtahnika Parva

This festival celebrates thrice a year, such as Ashadha, Kartika and Phalguna. The Nandisvara Ashtahnika is parva of Asadha, on that day, they worship the status of Arhats and during the celebration of Kartika they worship Meru Mountain, hence, it is called Panchameru Astahnika.

Chatur-masya

The festival start with Ashadha Ashtahnika and ends with Kartika Ashtahnika. The devotees spend their time in learning and meditation due to rainy season, and household followed the path of austerity and strictly practiced the code of conducts.

Dasa-lakshana Parva

It is a ten days celebration, starts with Panchami in the month of Bhadra-pada, and also called as paryashana. It is a festival of realize the true nature of the soul, by lead a ten virtues of ideal life. Those virtues are 1. Ksama(Tolerance), 2. Mardava (Humanity), 3. Arjava (straightforwardness), 4.Satya (truthfulness), 5.Sauca (Purity in body, mind and action), 6. Tapa (Penance), 7. Samyama (self-control), 8.Tyaga(Renunciation), 9. Akincanya (non-attachment) and 10. Brahma-Carya (celibacy), irrespective of men and women, they followed universal nature by faith. Jainas not aimed about material gain, but follow the religious prosperity.

Dipavali

The festival of Dipavali celebration is differ from Hindus. Jains considered this day as emancipation of Mahavira. The first teaching of Mahavira to his disciple is celebrated by burning torches on the first day of Kartika. Tamil Jainas also celebrating this festival by worship the Jina.

Gouri Nompi

This festival is celebrates by women, in the month of Bhadra-pada, the third of the bright fortnight. The meaning of Nompi and Gouri is festive and Hindu as well as Jaina deity respectively. Both Gouri and Isvera have been adapted in Jainism as deities of eleventh Thirthankara, sreyamsa, the womenfolk worship these goddesses for their husband's long life.

Jina-ratri

This festival is celebrate during the bright fortnight of Magha for commemorate the emancipation of the first Thirthankara Rishabha. The Hindus also celebrate this day as Siva-ratri and worship the deities in them and follow some of the path preached by them.[2]

Mahavira Jayanti

Generally, the birthday of Mahavira, the 24th Thirthankara celebrating as Mahavira Jayanti during the month of Chaitra. Even the Jainism obtains the name Jaina Dhara during his time, before that it identified by Arhat Dharma, Sramana Dharma. He considered as reviver of

Sramana Dharma and charity but Tamil Jains are celebrating this day differenly from above that they are preparing cradle and placing idols of Jina child in it.[3]

Moksha – saptami

This festival is celebrating on the month of Sravana for commemorate the day of Moksha by Parsvanatha on the Sammeta mountain in Bihar.

Nulu-hunnive

The meaning of Nulu-hunnieve is 'the full moon day of the thread'; it celebrated by theDigambaras of Karnataka. According to Jaina, tradition, the first emperor, of India, Bharata, created the varna of Brahmins and rewarded the holy men, he gave sacred thread, this thread wearing ceremony celebrating during the full moon day of Sravana, the importance of this ceremony is to protect the religion and philosophy for follow the path of the three jewels.

Ratna-traya Parva

This festival is celebrating thrice a year, during the thirteenth lunar day and full moon day of the months of Bhadra-pada, Magha and Chaitra by both recluses and lay people. It strengthened their belief of three jewels which are the foundation of the Jaina creed.

Sruta-Panchami

This is celebration of commemoration of the compilation of the Sruta (holy scriptures) observed day. According to tradition, Both Acharyas (Puspa-danta and Bhutabali) started to write and teach to Thirthankaras on A.D 156, before that all things are in oral formation. The compiled texts are known as Satkhandagama. The scriptures are considered as symbol of Samyag-jnana (right-knowledge) by Jainas, during this festival celebration they reverence the scriptures with great procession, and they arrange religious discourses to spread the right knowledge.

Vijaya-dasami

Vijaya-dasami is observed by both Hindus and Jainas. Jainas celebrated this festival during the tenth days of the bright fortnight of the month of Asva-yuja, but the connotation differs from Hindus. The Jinas worshipped Padmavati, the Yakshi of Parsva-nath Thirthakara instead of Hindu's Durga. A based on Hindu custom, they conducted animal sacrifice in eighthday, but the opposite way by Jainas, they celebrated this festival as Jiva daya-astami, the concept is avoid injury to any living beings and propagation of Ahimsa (Non-violence)

Vira-sasana Jayanti

According to traditions, this festival is celebrate in bright fortnight to Sravana and this day is commemorates of the first Vira-sasana, which means teaching of Lord Mahavira.

Yugadi

It is also called Ugadi in Kannada which is fall in the first day of the bright-fortnight of Chaitra of the Lunar calendar. Hindus also celebrate this festival, but the aim of celebrating this is by Jaina is to remember the Manus or Kulankaras (the patriarch) and Rishabha, the first of the Thirthankara. The Kulankaras were the pioneers of the ages called Susana-Dussama and Dussama-Sus. According to Jains belief that, it is the day of victory of the Emperor Bharata (son of Adi-natha or Rishabha) over fire continents and another important is that Mallinatha, the 19th Thirthankara entered his mother's womb. They are celebrating this for three-fold importance, during this day they perform special Poojas with co-religionists, offer charities to the needy and spread the gospels of the Thirthankaras.[4]

References

[1] A.Sreedhara Menon, A survey of Kerala History, (S.P.C.S), Kottayam, Kerala, 1970, p.89

[2] Ibid

[3] Jainamedu kal-parra, Sree Ananta-natha swami temple Golden Jubilee sourvenir, Kal-para,1983

[4] P.M.Joseph, Jainism in South India, The Internatioal School of Dravidian Linguistics, Thiruvanthapuram

CHAPTER FIVE

CONCLUSION

The Evil practice of Varna system gave birth to Jainism, and its principles put forward shock to ritualistic Vedic religion, and Brahmin domination violated by Jain's equality. Jaina religion gave importance to principle of Ahimsa and it most applicable to both human beings and animals, so it made Brahmanism reform itself.

The Jains keenly rejected the Sanskrit which patronized by Brahmins and promoted Vernacular language, instead of Sanskrit, the Jains used Prakrit to preach their principles and doctrines and wrote religious literature in Ardhamagadhi. The reason for the growth of Prakrit and its literature by the use of Vernacular language, same way the development of Marathi language led by the regional language of Sauraseni, along with these language Kanada also promoted by them and Jain literature enriched in various forms such as epics, puranas and drama.

Jainism enhances the art and architecture. They erected stupas, carved pillars and large statues. To give honour to saints they built stupas, the famous Jain sculptures are seen in Rajasthan, Madhya Pradesh etc... most popular were the huge statues of Gomateswar at Sravanabelgola and Karakal.

The Jains cut the rocks and turned as cave temples, it identified by Hatigumpha cave at Udayagiri in Orissa and similar in Junagarh, Osmanabad etc... The efficiency of Jain architecture and sculpture is reflected at Dilwara temple at Mount Abu in Rajasthan. They played marvelous pattern and extraordinary skill of masonry.

Brahmanical religion opposed the money transaction, but it supported by Jainism, it acted as a middlemen for exchange of manufactured goods, so many traders came to the fold of Jainism.

During 11th and 12th centuries, Jain arts reached its zenith and it could be find in temple and idols which still existing in various place such as, Mathura, Gwalior, Junagarh, Chittor, Abu and some of place in the district of Rajasthan, Madhya –Bharat, Bundelkhand, Mysore and Orissa, and it accepted as some of the best specimens of Indian Architecture and Sculpture, especially, the temple of Abu, the Chittorgarh's Jain-tower , Elephanta caves of Orissa and another important one is seventy feet idol of Gomateshwara or Bahubali in Mysore.

Jains came to Kerala for trade purpose during 3rd century BCE, first they reached Wyanad and spread to other parts which now exist in Kerala even today but are transformed as Hindu temple. Those are, The Matilakam and its vicinity area temple was main Jaina temple but it turned into Hindu temple. The Kudalmanikkam temple at Irinjalakuda, was Jaina temple and it converted into Hindu temple which dedicated to Bharta, the brother of Sri Rama. The old Jaina temple with natural rock cut came, contains image of Parswanatha, Mahavira and Padmavadi devi in Kallil near Perumbavur. Now a day it turned into Hindu Temple of Bhagavathi and Pooja's are conducting by Namboothiri Brahmins.

The Jain temples mostly converted into Hindu temples eventhough, Jains regular visit to these shrines and worshipping Jain God not Hindu God. Archaeological excavation critically analysed and studied about Jain monuments some of the rituals which Hindu are following now are really taken from practices of Jainism. Some of them are, Nagaradhana, Yaksha, Yakshni etc... A. Sreedhara Menon denoted that "Naga or snake worship which is popular in Kerala is the result of the impact of Jainism. Bhagavathi as a Hindu deity is also alleged to have been assimilated from the Jain Pantheon."

Jainism became popular in Kerala in 9th, 10th and 16th Centuries. Some of the prominent Jain centres in Palakkad are.... Jainamedu, Alathur, Mundur, and Parvassery. Currently only one Jain family is living in Jainamedu. Paruvassery Jain temple turned into Hindus temple named as Palliara and present generation not known the fact that it previously, Jain temple and they believe that, earlier it was a Buddhist temple. Sivalinga was properly maintained which was under Baniyan tree, but the Jains idols are not properly maintained. One more idol of the Jains present the Hindu people consider it as Kali.

In and around of Alathur has some of the Jain temples; the Pallikarnnu Jain Shrine has only stones but not maintained properly, so it scattered here and there. Kallam parambu- has Sivalinga under Baniyan tree, and ruined temples located in Chimbachala, and Godapuram's Shrine needs detailed study, but the details survey of Bhagavathi and Shiva shrine will reveal the real fact.

Mundur Ezharn Kota has one Jain temple in private land of a person named Divakaran. But there is not much information about those two granite idols of Thirthankara. Recently, the Jain temple regained its fame again, particularly; Swamy Bhuvanakirthi Bhatarak from Kanakarigi and Sri Jaina Math in Karnataka visited it. The

Jain shrine of Vijayapadman has now planned to renovated and maintain as ancient monument to preserve the concept of Jainism by maintaining a Jain Literature Library, and they held annual festivals and social activities based upon their customs and traditions.

The only family living at Jainamedu and they wants to shift their family to Karnataka before that they want to hand over their valuable books, maps, and details of Jainism to library.

The Government should take steps to preserve the Jain monuments throughout country and thereby make the students, and scholars, those who are interested in doing research about Jainism to get reliable materials.

Jain [illegible] of Vijayapura [illegible] is now [illegible] and [illegible] as ancient [illegible] to [illegible] the concept of [illegible] by [illegible] and they hold annual festivals and social activities [illegible] their customs and traditions.

[illegible] that they [illegible] that they [illegible] to [illegible] maps and [illegible]

[illegible] Government should [illegible] this [illegible] the [illegible] and [illegible] students and scholars, those who are interested in doing research about Jainism [illegible]

Glossary

Ahimsa : Non-Violence

Anekanta : Non- Absolution

Aneanta : Non-Violence

Aparigraha : Non-Possession

Asteya : Non-Stealing

Basati : Temple

Bhakti : Devotion

Bhaktimarga : Path of Devotion

Brahmacharya : Celebacy

Butha : Ghost

Ganadhara : Disciple

Chitta : Mind

Deva : God

Gana : Sect

Jiva : Being

Dharma : Religion

Karma : Action

Karma Marga : Path of Action

Karuna : Compassion

Maya : Delusion

Mukti : Salvation

Muni : An Ascetic

Pantha : Sect

Patigyraha : Possession

Pravrtti : Tendency

Rasa : Taste

Ratantraya : Three Jewels

Sampradaya : Sect

Samvibhaga : Equal Distribution of Wealth

Sanga : Sect

Samsara : World
Sadhana : Observance
Sadhaka : Way on the Path
Satya : Truthfulness
Sramana : Ascetic
Tirtha : Shrine/Holy Place
Thirthankara : Tirthankar
Varna : Color
Yajna : Sacrifices

Bibliography

BIBLIOGRAPHY

PRIMARY SOURCES

1. Cences Report-1926
2. Gazetteer of India, Kerala state Gazetter, Vol II, Part II, Thiruvanathapuram,1986.
3. Kerala District Gazetteer, Thiruvanathapuram, 1997
4. Malabar Gazetteer, Thiruvanthapuram,1997
5. South Indian Inscrition Vol V, No.784,1926
6. The Encyclopaedic District Gazetteers of India South Zone, Vol II, New Delhi, 1979 I
7. Journal of Indian History, Vol.XLVI, Part II, 1973
8. Bulletin of Ramavarma Research Institute, Part II, Trichur, 1937
9. Travancore Archaeological Series, Vol II, Part II, Trivandrum,1919
10. Encyclopaedia Britannica, Vol II, Britain, 1768
11. Websters New International Dictionary, London, 1928
12. Palakkad District Directory, Palakkad,1994

SECONDARY SOURCES

1. All India Chinmaya Yuva Kendra, Awakening Indians to India, Chennai,2003.
2. Batt,S.C (e.d.,), The Encyclopaedic District Gazetteers of India-South Zone, Vol II, New Delhi,1982
3. Bernier,M.Ronald., Temple Arts of Kerala, New Delhi,1982
4. Bhandarkar,R.G., Vaishnavism, Saivism and Minor Religious System, Delhi,1965

5. Brown,Lewis., This Believing World, New York,1961
6. Chandra, Ramesh (e.d.,) Religious of India, New Delhi,2004
7. Das, Mohan Ram (e.d.,) Jainism A Study, New Delhi,2000
8. Desai,P.B., "Jainism in Kerala" Journal of IndianHistory, XXXV,Part II, Trichur,1973
9. Dybois, J.A.Abbe., Hindu Manners, Customs and Ceremonies, New Delhi,1992
10. Gandhi M.K., The Story of My Experiments with Truth, Great Britain,1952
11. Gopalakrishnan,P.K., Jainamatham Keralathil, Thiruvanathapuram, 1974
12. Gopalakrishnan,P.K., Keralithinte Samskarika Charitram Thiruvanathapuram,1994
13. Gopinatha Rao, T.A.., Travancore Archaeological Series, Vol II, Part II, Trivandrum,1919
14. Ilango Adikal.,'Silappathikaram', Tran., Danieloo, London, 1967
15. Innes.C.A.(e.d)., Malabar Gazetteer, Thiruvanathapuram,1997 (Re-print)
16. Jaini, Chand Manak., Life of Mahaveera, Allahabad,1908
17. Jain Heerlal., Bharateeya Samskarathinu Jainamathinte Sambhavana, Tran., Trivandrum,1971
18. Jawaharlal, G,.Jainism in Andhra, Prakrita Bharat Academy, Jaipur,1994
19. Kareem.C.K., Kerala District Gazatteers-Palakkad, Eranakulam,1976
20. Kramrisch, Stella., The Arts and Crafts of Kerala, Cochin,1970
21. Krishna Menon, T.K., 'Malabar Temples' Bullettin of Rama Varma Institute, Vol V, Part II, Trichur,1937
22. Klien, Augsta., Legends and Myth of Spriritual India,

Delhi,1984

23. Kunjanpillai,P.N.Elamkulam., Kerala Charithrathinte Eruladanja Edukal, Thiruvanathapuram, 1963
24. Kurup,K.K.N., Aspects of Kerala History and Culture, Trivandrum,1977
25. Kurup,K.K.N.,The Cult of Teyyam and Hero-worship in Kerala, Calcutta,1973
26. Lal.B.B(e.d.,), Indian Archaeology-A Review 1969-70, Archaeological Survey of India, New Delhi,1970
27. Logan, William., Malabar Mannual, Vol I, Madras, 1951
28. Malayali.A.A(e.d.,), Palakkad District Directory, Palakkad,1994
29. Nandi,Ramendra Nath., Religious Institutions and Cult in the Deccan, Delhi,1973
30. Narayana Ayyar, E.V., Origin and Early History of Saivism in South India, Madras,1936
31. Narayanan,M.G.S., "New Light on Kunavayil Kottam and the Date of Cilappadikaram", XLVIII, Part III, Delhi,1970
32. Narayanan,M.G.S., Perumals of Kerala, Calicut,1996
33. Neelakanda Sastri,K.A., History of South India, Madras,1966
34. Ramachandran Nair, K.K (e.d.,) Gazetteer of India, Kerala State Gazetteer, Vol II, Part II, Thiruvanathapuram, 1919
35. Sahadevan,M., Towards Social Justice and Nation Making- A Study of Sahadaran Ayyappan, Trichur,1993
36. Sharma,R.S., Ancient India, Delhi,1990
37. Smith,A.Vincent., Oxford History of India (e.d.,), Percival Spear, London,1958
38. Sreedhara Menon,A., A Survey of Kerala History,Madras,1998
39. Thaper,Romila., A History of India, Delhi, Calcutta

40. Thripathy,R.S. History of Ancient India, Delhi,1942
41. Thomas,P., Festivals and Holidays of India, Bomaby,1971
42. Thomas,P., Hindu Religion Customs and Manner, Bombay,1975
43. Unnithan.N.G. Journal of Indian History, Vol XLVI, Part II, "Relics of Jainism-Alathur" Vanamalai, N.V., Studies in Tamil Literature, Madras,1969
44. Varier,M.R.Raghava., Ammavazhi Keralam, Kerala Sahithya Academy, Thrissur, 2006
45. Varier,M.R.Raghava., Keraleeyatha Charithramanagal, Vallathol Vidya Peedom, Sukapuram, 1990
46. Velayudan Panikkassery., Kerala Charitra Padanagal, Vol I, Kottayam, 1980
47. Vijayachandra Jaini, V.C., 'The Jain Temple at Palaghat' in Govt. Victoria College, Magazine, Vol.V, No.3, February 1939
48. Watters, Thomas., On Yuvan Chuvang's Travels in India, Delhi,1961

Appendix

THIRTHANKARAS AND THEIR SYMBOLS

No. Name of the Thithankaras Cognisance Tree

1 Adinatha (Rishabhanatha) Bull Banyan

2 Ajitanatha Elephant Sal

3 Sambhavanatha Horse Piyala

4 Abhinandhanatha Monkey Priyangu

5 Sumatinatha Curlew (Krauncha) Sal

6 Padmaparabha Red Lotus Chhatra

7 Suprasvanatha Svastka Priyangu

8 Chandraprabha Crescent Moon Naga

9 Suvidhinatha Makara Sali

10 Sitalanatha Srivatsa Priyangu

11 Sreyamsanatha Rhinoceros Tanduka

12 Vasupujya Buffalo Patali

13 Vimalanatha Boar Jambo

14 Anantanatha Falcon Asoka

15 Dharmanatha Thunder Bolt Dadhipama

16 Santinatha Deer Nandi

17 Kunthunatha Goat Bhilaka

18 Aranatha Nandyavarta Mango

19 Mallinatha Pitcher Asoka

20 Munisuvratanatha Tortoise Champak

21 Naminatha Blue lotus Bakula

22 Neminatha Conchshell Vetasa

23 Parsavanatha Snake Dhataki

24 Mahavira Lion Sal

Photos

Entrance of Jainamedu Temple,Palakkad

Chaddranatha Swamy Temple, Jainamedu,Palakkad (Old Statue)

Chaddranatha Swamy Temple, Jainamedu,Palakkad (Present Statue)

Juwalamuki Devi

24 Thirthankara Images

Jainamedu Temple –ruin monument (old status)

Jainamedu Temple –Present status

Printed by Libri Plureos GmbH in Hamburg,
Germany